The Sidewalk Motel

Poems from a Poverty Skola

and **PoShunary** (the Po' People's Dictionary)

a linguistically liberated glossary of
one kolonizer's language

Tiny Gray-Garcia

ISBN 978-1-956534-02-3

Thank you to POOR Press team
for design and copy-editing.

POOR Press is a poor and indigenous
people-led press dedicated to publishing the
books and scholarship of youth, adults, and
elders in poverty locally and globally.

**www.poormagazine.org
www.poorpress.net**

Stolen Land Tour photos on pages 22, 59, 61, 69, 73, and 92
by Brooke Anderson, @movementphotographer

Dedicated to my Disabled, Houseless, OG, Taino poverty skola Mama Dee, for without whom there would be no me... and no poetry... Uncle Al Robles and A. Faye Hicks (Po' Poet Laureate of POOR Magazine)—two of the best poverty skola poets I ever knew—My Sun Tiburcio, who walks with me in struggle & liberation, and all the houseless/landless, indigenous, disabled, incarcerated, swept, evicted and displaced warrior mamas who fight and struggle, steal and beg, in every crevice and corner to keep our kids in a bed...

Acknowledgements

I want to thank and appreciate the 1st nations warrior ancestors of this land, the Ohlone/Lisjan nation, who are still here 528 years later guiding this povertySkola spiritually and lovingly in so many ways and then to my POOR/Homefulness family of fellow houseless, indigenous, disabled poverty skolaz for without whom there would be no Homefulness MamaFested—who have given this houseless mama and daughter a roof, which enabled me to even be able to write—much less write poetry... I wanna lift up and thank my fellow welfare QUEEN badass Xingona Junebug Kealoha, a baaadass poet/shero poverty skola and my Mama Dee's other daughter. I wanna lift up my best friends, my brothers & sisStars for Lyfe and fellow baaadass Po' Poets Muteado SIlencio, Leroy Moore and Laure McElroy who I miss everyday, Aunty Frances Moore, Dee Allen, Israel Munoz, Queennandi XSheba, ViviT, Momi Palapas, Ingrid De Leon, Teresa Molina, Mama Rosellia, Corrina Gould, Fuifuilupe Niumeitolu, Pearl Ubungen, Angel Heart, Tenika Blue, Tony Robles, Joey Villareal, Min KingX and all the youth Skolaz at Deecolonize Academy, Papa Bear, POOR Magazine's Panhandler reporter, for teaching me so much about how to be a truth warrior poet journalist. Grateful Bear for encouraging and supporting me to even publish this collection.

To baadass artists and designers A.S. Ikeda and Maya Ram for all their amazing design skills and redistributed time to even make Poor PRESS happen, Asian Robles, Celia Espinosa for their amazing art, Paige Kirsten, a tech Shero and beautiful hearted person, Clemmy, Bridget, Amanda, Maya, and Jess Hoffman for linguistically liberating some of my 6th-grade edumakated colonial words and for all of the ancestors of all this pain who walk with us everyday in this stolen land. Ometeotl, ASE, Ahoooo.

Contents

I am a poverty skola

I am a poverty skola
That houseless mama
That houseless daughter

All those people you don't want to see
Never want to be
Look away from me
What you gonna do
arrest me?

I'm in your cit-eee

I am a poverty skola
And I rock my jailhouse attire cuz me and my po' mama did
    jail time for the poverty crime of
Being houseless in this occupied indigenous Holla

I am a poverty skola
The melanin-challenged daughter of a strong Afro-BoriKen
    Mama
For without whom there would be no me...
A Mama soltera
And a welfareQUEEN

(My Slam Bio—the way we introduce ourselves in the Po' Poets Project of POOR Magazine)

Introduction

*Anti-Social Workers and Case Manglers call me
Crazy, Lazy, Dumb and a Bum cuz my knowledge
dont come from the Institu-SHUN...*

I was told multiple times by akkkademiks and anti-social
workers that "I could not write." or writing was not a
"sensible" career move when I was on hell-fare (welfare
crumbs). In large part this was bcuz I never mastered
the linguistically dominant rules of punkkktuation and
grammar.

At age 11 me and my mama became houseless and I had to
drop out of formal institutions of learning so I could work
and help my disabled mama and me survive. I enrolled
full-time in the skoo of hard knocks, where I like to add
I graduated wit a PhD in poverteee. My Xingona warrior,
indigenous, disabled, poverty skola Mama Dee was my
writing teacher. Mama was a "G" and not user-friendly
or easy on me and if she didn't like something I wrote she
would crumple it up into a tiny ball and throw it at my head,
and her biggest "compliment" was "not bad" which she
rarely said. But she was insistent that the AristoKrazy didn't
own writing, history, art, poetry, theory and story-telling
and that it was extremely important for poor, indigenous
and houseless, "uneducated" people like us to take that
lie back and write beautiful poetry and prose about our
struggles and our lives. This is for you, Mama.

Thank you always, for everything and this poetry book and
PoShunary is dedicated to you—for without whom there
would be no me.

Part 1

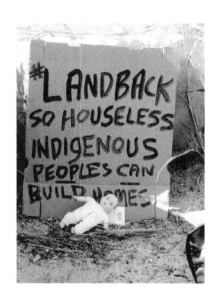

Lowrider Lecturer

Angel Baby, my Angel Baby
Oooooh, I love you, oooh I do
No one could love you like I do.
The lowrider lecturer presents his thesis on
the back seat of a Chevy Impala
the words sail thru the sky and out the narrow institutional
    skoo window
refusing to be caught by the mandate of white supremacist
    TESTS—
the story that only some people can b teachers while others
    are set for arrest

The Cholo Docta has letras behind his name that sway and
    sashay
to the sounds of War and Frankie Valli

When i hear the Cholo Docta my corazon skips a beat
cuz he teaches that the knowledge is within us—our
corazones—our almaz—puro amor—our hands—our feet—
our work—our struggle—La vida Loca and the institution
can meet

The Cholo Docta brings medicine to the minds of all of us
caught in the trauma of colonization and gregorian time—
to my boricua ghetto-fabulous mama who was told she was
nothing—and could be nothing and no matter wit refused
to believe their pinche lies

the Cholo Docta is yo mama—your uncle, yo abuela—your
street corner preacher, your gardener—your dishwasher and
lives in your own mind

the lowrider lecturer delivers lecturaz in poesia and musica and prayer and dreams

The lowrider lecturer is busy—he and she are mixing their trajectories and developing their newest canons while they wash your dishes, mow your lawn and make your burrito with beans—

they are having their think tanks and their test prep sessions in front of the home depot and if u want to pass the test called life you better listen carefully to their lecturaz cuz they don't have time to repeat them or say them twice

between holding down three and four jobs caregiving for your babies, struggling with false borders and fake notions of who is a skola and who is a teacher for life

dedicated to Dr. Loco aka Jose Cuéllar y Luis Rodriguez y mi padrastro Virgil W.

Silenced before we speak

Sorted, separated, segregated, occupied—
intimidated
silenced before we speak,
teach, or write—
because we talk in tongues
considered dumb
—not right—
not proper and
therefore permanently kept an outsider.
They call it linguistics,
we built our own languages
they missed it
these are our tongues—our songs—
long ago written,
already sung—
from our elders—from our young—
indigenous cultures culled
from years past—
always put last—
stolen—beaten—taken down—
this theft is our legacy—
from a racist genocide called missionaries, formal
        education, and occupation
perpetuated throughout herstory
the loss of our myths and stories, language and glory . . .
Pidgeon, ebonics, nawat, zulu, tagalog, urdu, masagua
Take your pick
we have created complicated alphabets—
u get paid with fellowships to study, learn, archive and re-do
And then sort us out with your tests
When we don't/can't/won't speak like the man—

u call us illiterate—
At-risk—
Inept
BAM
The prison doors close
The systems choke
We are outside
On the side
Forever silenced
Relegated to a spoke
In yo wheel

Living off yo deal
Forced to steal
Back
What was ours to begin with

The Privilege of Breathing

As you sit under your roofs
And complain about the soot
Watching Air Quality Index
Soar to the roof
I must remind all of you living in places
So you can shelter in safety
of so many of us still outside
Evicted behind the lie of rent—the myth of success
The hoarding of stolen mama earth & all those real eSNAKE
    papers and payments
Hiding in doorways, car seats, bus benches
Without a place—away from your sheltered eyes
While Mama Earth fires rage outside
And you close your windows and doors
Heeding the warnings of sheltering in place for sure
So many of us can barely breathe no longer having the
    privilege
Of sheltered safe space
In the colonial terror launch centuries ago—
Poor people made poor by colonial theft and the lie of
    ownership
Continue to slip in and out of your fake lie called
    Non-profiteering
And Business Improvement Districts
The Privilege of Breathing
Shelter Beds and vouchers
Saviors and Charity complex
Black and Brown PoLice Terror
leading to Black and Brown PoLice Murder
And then there is the LIE OF RENT
And once again we are all left to ask

How do you shelter in place when you have no place?
How do you housed peoples/politricksters continue to
    practice the violent act of looking away?
I don't want your pity
I don't want your crumbs
I want to close a door, shut a window and share the privilege
    of breathing one more day to come

Enabling the kkkolonial
"Savage" and wealth-
hoarding wite-ness while
thousands of us are swept,
evicted & homeless

– *Podcast from a
povertyskola on spreaker /
ITunes*

We walk back and forth in a jailhouse every day

We walk back and forth in a jailhouse every day—it's called
    your doorways
tent cities
Bus benches
Metal chairs in the emergency room
waiting to be seen…

it's main street outside the razor wire plantation in a cell
    called houselessness and poverty
Teetering on a colonized definition of safety
from ugly laws to CONservatorSHIP
we can barely survive one day without the theft of our
    belongings, Cages, poLice Calls & fifty-one fifteeees

me daughter of a houseless, single mama—
sleeping on street corners, cars and not-really-public parks
    in this stolen indigenous territory
it's enough to drive anyone completely craz-eee
it took my mama—
unable to unhinge from that deep well of trauma

So what's the answer—
you don't want to see me
You would like to walk down the street cloaked in your
    American lie that doesn't include me

Yes we are political prisoners—
outside the razor wire plantations
us po' folks are NEVER free
not free from our mind demons

the abuse we can't get out our mind no matter the quantity
    of psycho-pharma-cology

I hold my mama in this space
rolling over her torture
everyday...
"My life is political
my prison is personal," she would always say

My struggle/our struggle is poetry
and i can't escape these walls inside my mind...
I can't ever be free
No Matter what
i can't ever be free

Private property is a settler lie

Private property def: refers to a system that allocates particular objects like pieces of land to particular individuals to use and manage as they please, to the exclusion of others and to the exclusion of any control by society.

Private Def: belonging to or for the use of one particular person or group of people only.

From the settler Lie of discovery to the settler lie of private proper-teee

To amerikkklan scarcity models causing us all to be in Pov-ver-tee—

Everything is a lie when trying to shield the

cult of hoarding, land stealing and I got MINES

This is the church

in the stolen land of I, I, & I

So when I'm talking bout liberation, reclaiming and Mama Earth taking back—we ain't speaking bout—re-oppressing mama earth—with more ownership Smack—

That's what got us here in the First F-in place—

melanated peoples believing the lie that ownership means you safe—indigenous peoples believing the lie that ownership means we liberate—homeless peoples believing that—ownership means we homeful

IF we don't want to re-oppress, reEvict re-desecrate our communities, our ancestors and Mama Earth—let's actually walk a different way

that has no roots in the colonizers sway

From West Huchuin to West Papua—the Settler lie of private property gives the devil-opers their way—

Gives the Real ESNAKKES more bloodstained paper to pay—

Today's poem from a poverty skola—goes out to all the peoples thinking thru this moment and how not to do emulate colonizers and owners—how to reclaim, lift UP and NEVER buy, sell and poison

NEVER buy sell and Poison—

precious mama earth again…

A Poem for Papa Bear

An Unknown Souljah Killed in the Undeclared War on the Poor

A thumb is a terrible thing to waste
Black, poor and disabled thumbs legs and lives
are perceived as trash when u live outside

after all we are not human in your eyes
just an "unsightly" tribe—
lost our humanity & persona-alities on the curbs, inside
    of doorways
and on the road-side

Excuse me sir—do u have any spare change?
On hard cement working cement aisles of objectified hate—

Here lies the Unknown Souljah—
Killed in the Undeclared War ON the Poor
standing on street corners, working cardboard and cups
maybe a blink of your eye gets us a sliver of your
    disgust-filled love

My Name is Papa Bear—did 3 tours in your empire wars—
killing people you never had to see, think about or care for
Now I'm houseless in these stolen United Snakes streets

Right in front of your eyes
and yet i exist nowhere
the only people who see me
are people who hope i disappear

Receiving 260 citations and now jail because you see me
    as trash

because you called the poLice instead of listen to my ask—

I died
I'm no longer there
only exist as a memory in your cluttered past

Here lies the UnKnown Souljah killed in the Undeclared
    War ON the poor
I was killed from the violence of your not wanting me here

Who Dies on Their Feet?

Ode to my sisSTAR welfareQUEEN—Mama Laure
McElroy—miss u every FUKING day

Our hearts cracked open in places too hard to still see
long ago lost in doorways, couches we slept in, places we
　　held mama in—trauma you might not believe
we hold this pain close—and don't scream—show Up and
　　show out for jobs, protests, meetings & movement
　　stra-te-gee

this was you beautiful sister-comrade Lau-reee—
calm, humble—rarely wanting to be seen—highly
　　functioning to the world—holding on by the fingernails
　　inside of seas of disguises
itching to shriek—
writing verse from Creator—poetry to sing

holding the broken hearts of your mama's mama—and my
    mama Dee—
you and i are so alike u said on thursday—broken in all the
    unseen places—yet working so hard too hard just to be

Just one more day we say in broken-ness
—and then we are there
in the world—holding everyone else up—
so we don't have to fall ourselves—
but we r falling
deep and far down the side
not able to get footing inside the kkkolonized mountain
    of lies

the separation nation—
the isolation river so wide

Where is the healing—
Where is it safe
I don't want to keep living
Oh but there's movement work and more people to lift up
    every day—
There are more people to hold
beyond just me and you

We perpetrate violence against our own bodies—all over
    the world
who needs the police when u got your own terror
falling so perfectly prey to kolonized offers
of ways to feel ok

So this offer stands comrades,
in Laure's honor

for her mama Caroline
and my Mama Dee
don't let us not see

this poem is in honor of my beautiful sis-STAR, writer,
    poet, hardcore revolutionary fighter for everyone else
    but herself—Lau-reeee
all of us broken revolutionaries in need of some love

who are saving mama earth—poor mamas, daughters and
suns but can't save ourselves

This prayer-poem is for u sister Laure and for my mama and
your mama—and all of us in between—i love u more than i
can say—

> *Would rather die on my feet, than live on my knees.*
> *—Emiliano Zapata*

Las Calles

(para Luis Demetrio Gongora Pat)

The Streets have so many colors
the colors have so many memories
memories of streets you are no longer on—
but wish you could be

Las calles tienen tantos colores
los colores tienen tantos recuerdos
Recuerdos de calles en las que ya no estás
pero desearían que estuvieras

The color of people who are no longer there
who we wish we could see
because they were removed by people who were scared
of what they could not contain, incarcerate or bear

El color de las personas que ya no están allí
a quien desearíamos poder ver
porque fueron eliminados por las personas que tenían miedo
de lo que no pudieron contener, encarcelar o soportar

19th & Shotwell are two of those streets
who meet inside of so much grief
the colors of loss of sounds and hands you no longer see

19th y Shotwell son dos de esas calles
que se encuentran dentro con tanto dolor
los colores de la pérdida de sonidos y manos que ya no ves

it was at this corner among peoples like me—those of us
    struggling with poverty

where state sanctioned guns
triggered by fear were called in to take away life
by laws and lies that were dangerously unclear

*en esta esquina entre gente como yo, los que luchamos contra
   la pobreza*
donde el estado sancionó las armas de fuego
*desencadenado por el miedo fueron llamados para quitar
   vida*
por leyes y mentiras peligrosamente confusas

Red the color of Mayan earth—a Mayan heart—of a father,
husband, worker, Sun, remnants that lived under hard-
working fingernails of a peaceful man named Luis lost to
poLice murdering Guns

*Rojo, el color de la tierra maya, un corazón maya, de un
padre, esposo, trabajador, sol, restos que vivieron bajo las
uñas trabajadoras de un hombre pacífico llamado luis
perdido por el asesinato de pistolas policiales*

Blue the color of the sky when the guns took you away into
a spirit where you live today

*Azul el color del cielo cuando las armas te llevaron y
transformaron en el espíritu en el que vives hoy*

White like the huipiles of your wife, daughter and mama—
white like the fear of the people who call the police on us
because they believe that we need to be saved.

Blancos como los huipiles de tu esposa, hija y madre, blancos como el miedo de la gente que llama a la policía porque creen que debemos ser rescatados

Green like the paper dollars needed to stay inside—and then, sometimes we are a little more safe

Verde, como los dólares en papel necesarios para permanecer encerrados, y así, a veces sentirnos un poco más seguros

Grices comò un sidewalk cuando usted recycled, lived, dreamed, played, walked—and waited for the pain to stop

waited to go home to another place across these killer colonizer borders painted in the sand

Grices comò la acera cuando reciclabas, vivias, soñabas, jugabas, caminabas —y esperabas que el dolor se detuviera

esperando para ir a casa, a otro lugar a través de estas fronteras colonizadoras y asesinas pintadas en la arena

These streets hold so many colors like small unseen paint brushes moving in the wind—they hold sounds too—like one that never leaves—no matter how many times they scrub us out—rub us out—take us down—pretend we were never here—

Estas calles tienen tantos colores como pequeños pinceles invisibles que se mueven con el viento, que retienen sonidos, como uno que nunca se va, sin importar cuántas veces nos limpien, nos froten, nos bajen, fingiendo como si nunca estuvimos aquí—

and there is one special sound—the one that is you—i see u
Luis—you are here and always will be

*y hay un sonido especial, el que eres tú, te veo Luis, estás aquí
y siempre estarás*

These streets and their colors so far from your origin ache
for u everyday—ache and break and listen for your return

for you to b ok

*Estas calles y sus colores tan alejados de su origen, duelen
por ti todos los días, duelen y rompen y escuchan tu regreso
algún día*

Ode to George Floyd

A poverty skola in amerikkklan (wit a
message for abolitionists everywhere

There are so many moments in that murderous day
Has this poverty skola mama feeling all types of ways
Which must be spoken—
Not silenced for the simple kkkort & CorpRape media
    takeaway

The corner sto—
The Blood-stained 20 dollar
The worker poverty skola behind the counter
Just covering it cuz that's how we skolaz take care
of each other
And the unspoken recognition that George Floyd
Like so many of us poLice terror victims
Was a poverty skola

The call to the kkkilers—the poLice
The lice on the Po
Who arrive with guns—
Cuz that's what krapitalism demands
So blood-stained dollars can CONtinue to flow

From human to human—
Without hesitancy
Without thinking
Without questioning
So life itself has a price—
Locked in wit so many PoLice kkkulture Lies

So evil can lurk inside
Ghosts with names like Chauvin and Mellone
Called to "take care of" Houseless, Disabled and poor
Humans lives with murdering tools; Guns and Tasers and
ChokeHolds

Black, Brown, indigenous Disabled fathers and Suns and
Brothers and Uncles—humans colonized behind so many
lies about poverty, trouble and other

Poverty scholarship is the over-standing that we poor
people aren't always ok—that our trauma bleeds into
conversations, cement streets—corner stores, shopping
carts, substance use and our own colonial destroyed roots

That goals and dreams were long ago lost to so many of us—
and now there is a killer around every corner called a kkkop
dropping a dime on us—for not living into that fake success
model called the amerikkklan dream

None of these are mistakes—they are krapitalist dreams,
nightmares—and warnings—we r all loaded up with from
an early age—

That no matter how many times we poverty skolaz try
we just can't make

This Poem is in honor of Mamaz / Este Poema es en honor a las madres

The "anthem" I wrote for the welfareQUEENs theatre production—dedicated to my fellow QUEENs Vivian, Junebug, Queenandi, Tracey, Dharma, Mama Blue, Pearl, Aunty Frances, Audrey CandyCorn and my sisSTAR Laure and especially my Mama Dee—for without whom there would be no me

(Espanol sigue)

This poem is in honor of mothers…
Houseless mothers and poor mothers
Low-wage mothers and no-wage mothers
Welfare mothers
And three-job-working mothers
migrante/indigenous mothers
And incarcerated mothers

in other words
this poem is honor of
DHS-ed with,
CPS-ed with and
Most of all
system messed with
mothers

This poem is honor of all those poor women and men
And yes I said men cause don't sing me that old song
About gender again

Who fight and struggle
And steal and beg
in every crevasse

And corner to keep our kids in a bed
Who dress and feed with tired hands
Who answer cries over and over again

This poem is in honor of all of us
Mothers who deserve to be coddled
And loved,
Fed and protected
Instead of criminalized,
Marginalized
and rarely respected

Who can barely make it but always do
And still raise all the world's people
Like me you and you

Can I get a witness?
This poem is honor of mothers
Who can barely make it but sometimes do
And still raise all the world's people
Like me, and you and you

(En Espanol)
Este Poema es en honor a las madres

Este Poema es en honor a las madres...
Madres Desamparadas y madres pobres
Madres con bajos salarios y sin salarios
Madres de Bienestares
y madres que trabajan tress jales
Madres Migrantes
y madres encarceladas
en otras palabras
este poema es en honor a
MIGRA-nisadas
(CPS) molestadas
y mas que nada
madres
attakadas por el systema
Este poema es en honor a todos esos hombres y mujeres
y si, dije hombres tambien porque no me cantes esa vieja
    cancion
sobre genero otravez
Quien pelean y luchan

y roban y ruegan
en cada brecha
Y esquina para mantener a sus hijos en una cama
quienes visten y dan de comer con manos cansadas
Quienes responded gritos una y otra vez
Este poema es en honor para esas
madres quienes se merecen un apapacho
y amor
Alimentacion y protecsion
En vez de ser criminalizadas
Marginadas
y rara la vez respetadas
Quienes apenas pueden sobrevivir pero siempre lo hacen
y todavia crean toda la gente de el mundo
Como yo, tu y tu.
Quien puede ser testigo?
Este poema es en Honor pa' las Madres
Quienes apenas pueden sobrevivir y aveses pueden
y crean toda la gente de este mundo
como yo y tu y tu.

CPS—APS—all the Ssses

CPS—APS—all the Ssses
That lead to our babies stolen, arrested & even death-es
Mamas, papas, don't show yo real feelings
Of sorrow or distresses
Don't admit to poverty or Homelessnesses

No mandated reporters here
Rooted in racist classist principles of fear
The Lie of ghettoization
And separation Nation—
Each seizure of our babies is blood-stained dollaz for the
Colonial Domination

the Juvenile NeverJustices
Foster & kkkort systems
Poor babies—poor mamaz—
Poor daddies—don't cry
The anti-social workers
The judges don't lie
Everyone gets paid
They all salivate
More Money waits
For another family to break...

Bad Choices

How DO you look away?

Because we houseless and poor people have been consistently referred to as the other—those people—it's our fault—our choices—and we are NOT OK—

The Homeless people—you call us—disembodying our humanity—like we are an "evil" tribe with no land or culture or purpose of life—

We have MADE BAD CHOICES—and therefore—somewhere in the back of yo mind—

Deserve to Die—OutSide

Admit it—

This isn't a trick

It's the REAL-EST ish ….

And where was that choices list?

Who wrote this unseen manual we all supposed to overstand & get

Who has the publishing rights—? God? Ancestors? Great Spirit?

BAD CHOICES CHOICES—these are Neo-liberal
narratives allowing u to hoard, profile, convict and evict
without missing a step.

Cleaning and Sweeping—Incarcerating and Taking—From
Belongings to Homes—we have no value to own, hold, love
or be slow—

Because we made BAD CHOICES—so goes the submersion
of our collective voices—our differences—our multitude
of lives

Today's PoemCast from a Poverty Skola—is dedicated to
all of us distinctly different, humans who happen to live
outside—the Bad Choice-makers—the losers, the low-lifes
and the bums in yo eyes
the Ones—who make you sick
cause you can't solve us
and of course We—are a monolith

Devil-opers and Real Esnakkkes

Making bloody colonial paper while ancestors lives are at stake

Maps drawn, treaties, promises broken and long gone
contracts and leases steal and extract like leeches
We have parking lots and condos to sell—
We have business deals—
come on take yo krapitalst pill—
5,700 years old—
Who really cares
There is money to make—and more of mama earth to steal
Sacred Shellmounds
What is that anyway?
Get out of the way
we can give u a plaque or street name
Get out of the way
Money stops for no-one—didn't u hear

I hear the gritos—I hear the screams—Ohlone Lisjan
mamaz with babies—under this violent asphalt veneer—
right here—they calling—like George Floyd murdered by
the same settler colonial poLice terror—like mamaz and
Suns and daughters in Sheikh Jarrah—like mamas in West
Papua, mamas in Kashmir—like mamas in the back of
poLice cars and in tents being swept like we aren't even here
They came
The devil-opers—and real esnakkkes—the parking lot
builders and the Condominium sellers—the speculators
said to the mamas—you don't belong here—so we gonna
re-write the game
The Mac store—and Old Navy—that's your new name
creating so many CONfusing disguises indigenous herstory
is washed from our gaze

41

Said no one's here—
Told and sold lies—created paper knives—they called Maps
And Contracts
And then kept on selling and re-telling—until everyone
Believed it like it was Fact—But the shift is upon us family—
the lies are being seen—the fake HIS-stories are falling into
Ohlone Lisjan rivers and streams

they calling us all So Keep lifting up the Her-STORIES of
truth all these mamaz—
all these babies—all of our ancestor graves—
From West Berkeley Shellmound to Sheikh Jarrah—no
more lies can b sold and told—From West Papua to West
Oakland—Mama Earth must be UnSEttled and UnSold
EVERY FUKING Day

Dedicated to the ancestors of the West Berkeley Shellmound
and their descendants still here fighting and not giving up

On Poor People Feet & Teeth

Mixed race, poverty skola mama used to say…
Only way they know u Po' is your teeth and feet—all fuked
    up and cray
otherwise your code switch disguise is complete
Cuz u look wite
so to the wite supremacist world we live in
you alright

Lost most of my teeth in wars against us Poor
Cheap, sugar-filled food,
endless stress
And no free dental care in poor people hellthcare

Born with disabled feet—
Pigeon toed they called it
hyper-flexible, no padding on the bottom
—like a bird wit his beak
Barely could walk—without falling—
unbearable pain was always calling
Doc told me its my one DNA marker for my Taino
peeps—made worse with bad shoes, free shoes, standing all
    day and night to hustle for underground work and food
Over-priced surgery never an option
Jus kept walking in pain—
pain I just had to walk on

Mama would say these and other things poor folks live wit
    everyday
sometimes the pain from head to toe gets so great
It's not ok
But then mama would add

Get used to it wite gurl—be glad u standing at all
got to hustle that paper
no time to b sad

Fast forward to 2019
Teaching young houseless & formerly houseless youth—
they can become doctors too—learning from their mamas,
uncles and aunties like Mama rosella and Mama Juju
But also seizing wite-science in Skoo
To inflitrate the paper knowledge and help us po' folks by
providing actually free healing-care

The Tenderloin Take

The TL—where there used to be Brown & Black Faces
In every one of these beautiful places

Now there are barely traces
after the sharp Knife of Displacement
cuts us out -
Throwing us on the pavement

Gentrification has hit
Where Art isn't any SAFER
Where Snow Storms are born
Removing & Displacing
Poor peoples of ALL races

the Tenderloin
Last Poor People Frontier
But NEVER fear
The kkkolonizers are HERE

Take Long looks
Our Herstories aren't in the
Arkkkives and His-STORY books

Our stories, Our Lives
are Breathing, Screaming, Crying,
Get Me Out Of Here…

This aint an exhibit
Or Art installation
No Fetishized Grant Dance HERE

Our evictions, Our Addictions
And Then...
Mysterious Fires Appear

A few of us remain
Holding on by a thread
Screaming out our Forgotten Names

Until the thread breaks
and the Spekkk-u-LATERs
Get out their Rakes

Building condos, hospitals and
cafes with all the money our broken bodies
can make

The eugenicists won wit this one

(for my mama & all the mixed light-brites still to come)

The eugenicists won wit this one

I am the Suckkksess at the end of the melanin test

Now my Black and Brown ancestors whose only wish was
that I was witer than them

Can Rest

The eugenicists Won wit this one—

seen by some as wite

like the plantation walls

we all run from

The eugenicists sed birth out the black & only then u will
be safe

no longer fall in all the crackkker jack spaces

Mixed Race Mama left by her mama—hated from the day
she was born—beat into pulps of fear—over & over—

called names bout her hips & lips—& her beautiful light
Black form

torn into pieces by the no-ones that ever protected her or
ever saw her born

47

i held her pain in my small arms

tried to heal with all my child heart

U see mama got wit robert redford look-a-like cuz
whiteness was rightness & she thot at least me would be out
of harm—

her & pilgrim dad had me & made the eugenicists happy—

birthed out all the color—flowed it back into the earth,
Yemaya, mama Ocean—the stars & the beautiful black sea

One day mama couldn't go on anymore—cried until she
had no mo tears left in her heart or soul—i tried so hard to
make it ok—But never cd—still hold her with everything i
have & all the other mamaz who are sad—still barely creep
across the floor some days can't seem to shake it or really
stand

I live in the gray place of incomplete identity

people don't over- under- or inner-stand me

my heart is brown like the fresh earth and black like night
and the deepest part of the sea—

Where u just hold on cuz u alive in any form

praying every day to ancestors from all four corners who
still live in me

The Displacement of Love

I lost so many blankets, toasters, baby pictures and
remnants of my heart when i was displaced.

I lost whispers, hugs and my mama's tired hands.

I lost best friends' phone numbers, my sun's art, my art,
poetry, laundromats, and my favorite corner store.

I lost my best friend, my lover and my bus stop,

I lost my room, my window, the moon and myself—

I have been evicted & displaced so many times i can't even
remember who,

but this last time, i lost you...

Happy Houseless Mamas Day???

When People Say
Happy Mama's Day
it just never felt ok
When so many mamas & babies sit behind false borders and
    steel bars,
sleeping in tents and cars,
Dreaming of their lost babies shot by PoLice fire
No equity, No Money,
Not time to love or spit bars
Hold their babies in their arms
Dream Dreams or Gaze at stars
Our Communities and support and life lost to
    gentriFUKED streets
Our ideas and dreams so often Silenced so we can
    barely speak

Happy Mama's Day…
How can it really be—
anything more than Amerikkklan Hypocrisy

How bout Equity, Healing-Care Not Hellth-Care
How bout Housing, De-carceration and the end of PoLice
    Terror of our Suns and Daughters and the War on the
    POOR

Happy Mama's Day
How can it be
Until all of our Mamas & Mama Earth can b free
Otherwise isn't Happy Mama's Day just more krapitalist
    HypoKRAZY?

Paper bags made of memories

Side by Side
chair frames and baby toys,
jackets, toothbrushes coffee cans and pillows
wrapped up in paper bags made of memories

nylon homes buried under lives made of storms
these aren't the storms of rain and thunder
sleet or hail—these rain drops include sheriff's boots
and eviction notices,
this thunder is made of the sound of your home bouncing
    on the pavement
the lightning is a po'lice flashlight shining car windows
and hail-filled slices of
foreclosure

humans walking softly on mama earth
permanently outside

No Matter how Many times you Sweep me, Incarcerate me
    or study me, it doesnt give me a home...

Poverty Scholarship

Anthropology,
Ethnography
Psychology

The study about us
Without us
Our spirit,
Our cultures
Our languages
Our traditions
Through your lens,
Your frame
Your perspective
Fetishized
Researched
Deconstructing our struggle
Figuring us out while our communities are dismantled and
    in rubble
Funded by fellowships
Acquired with academic privilege.
Linguistic domination gifts
Long ago parsed out to the sorted and separated

Who excelled in amerikkkan skoool systems, formal
institutions of learning, the myth of inclusion and the cult
of independence

How you gonna take photographic essays of gente pobre in
Nicaragua, Arkansas and Bangladesh

But not give them so much as a slice of your

Privilege,
equity
and access
How you gonna fly
Back to your lands,
Your publishers
Your nests
With warm feelings
of 21st century colonizers,
our stories
and a good grade on your thesis and final tests

Sooooo I have a new plan
It's called sharing the wealth
Accreditation and linguistic domination
Mess

Flipping the hierarchy
Of who is an expert, scholar
Who does the picture-taking, story-making
And who gives the tests

Mamalaure, jewnbug, Gloria, teresa, queennandi, marlon, tony, bruce, jasmine, tibu vivien, muteado, israel, dee, me, and gente pobre the world over hold the knowledge, of survival, struggle, thrival to create a new kind of fellow-ship that is rooted in all of our gifts

It's a SisterShip, a BrotherShip, an AuntieShip and a MamaShip

It's a new non-colonizing, non-hierarchical, equity-sharing tip—called poverty scholarship—

Sterile

Excerpt from a PoemOlogue Theatre series by PovertySkola

How is it
That some of us are unfit,
And some of us are fixed
Some of us are labeled sick
While others held and kissed

Over 20,000 houseless/poor women forcibly sterilized
terrorized,
Locked up
shut
Never seen
silently killed
By WITE-science helllth-care teams

Feeble-minded-defective-crazy-dumb
These words like knives—permanently mutilating
    thousands of poor women's tongues

Steel cages built with eugenicists' pens behind akademiks'
    doors
Writing violent numbers down on paper folders—
Naming us with codes and chains
And permanently locking multiple doors

Now they wipe and scrape us off of
Streets
Call them sweeps
Same program
Different broom
Same laws

Same Krapitalist cause
Meant to kill us all

I got Mines—the Amerikkklan Dream Blues...

In the system—based on "pay"
Our tired bodies are used for trade

We think to ourselves
If only we could get "made"
If only we could get paid

But the funny piece
About that Belief
Is that every dream rooted in acquisition
is a dream rooted in dominance and oppression

Every dream rooted in gettin it in
Is a day spent in another poor person being done in

Every moment spent in I got to get mines
Is someone else's stolen life

I got those amerikkklan dream blues
Where revolutionary moves get lost
In the holes of our too tight broken sole shoes

Every day spent barely covering the rent
Is another day lost to Mama Earth Dominance

Is another day away from what we can do to step away
From buying, selling, our bodies, her body and our souls
Based on how much we can pay

This PoemCast from a Poverty Skola goes out to my fellow
poverty skolaz (and un-colonizing wealth hoarders) who

feel lost in the broken krapitalist dreams that always costs—
prices rise—and can't ever seem to be bought—

Crossing false borders, losing lives and limbs, working for
shit, doing criminalized labor until we get pinched—and
yet what happens—do we EVER get ahead??? Liberation
can't be the answer until we overstand how we all got this
krapitalist cancer.

We Can't live into being free—unless we can all see—that
the answer isn't in Getting our piece

While the akademiks and wealth-hoarders study, exploit
and profit off our pain—continuing to gain their comfort
based on our struggle to attain—

We are still lost—behind those border walls—those
        prison Cells
Those Buy My Ugly House Poster Boards

While our dream continues to be—I just need to get paid
        and hoard
Or I will never be Free
We will be stuck in I got Mines
Black and Brown Krapitalism ain't the answer fam
It's just another wite supremacist lie

Part 2

Photo by Brooke Anderson | @movementphotographer

Cuz the colonizer is u

Colonizers don't all come with pockets sewn on with colonizer dollaz...

colonizers come in all shapes, sizes and colors. spewing words like healing, art and I'm here to help release your inner child

age-grade separated schools & therapy to take you away from their colonizer named problems like yo ancestors, traditions, spirit & knowledge

Colonizers turn struggle into a pill that can heal—medicine into a product and feeling good into poison wit names like whiskey and beer

transform indigenous traditions, communities of color voices, sacred land, into gangsta rap, pocohontas, shopping malls & white supremacist notions of fear

—coming to you to solve your colonizer created problems with substances, not EVER affordable housing and parties— taking you out your pain & make you unable to live in your head

Face creams, and lotions to keep you in stasis so u won't deal with natural reality like aging

Telling u we have a potion for that annoying feeling like missing yo babies, yo uncles, ancestors and yo mama—

sucking u in and turning u out wit dreams of buying and selling mama earth to be happy while they b devil-oping your ancestors' burial spaces—

CON-fusing u so much you sell out yo own grandma

so u walk into old navy and buy something they tell u will make u look more sexy which is necessary if u believe that their blood-stained dollaz are actually more than just paper

and then one day when u drunk up all their poison, discarded yo colonizer defined problems, devil-oped your barrios, sacred land & lost everything that's real & true

—you look around and realize now...

the colonizer is you

Photo by Brooke Anderson | @movementphotographer

The Sidewalk Motel

One poem conflicts with another poem
it sounds like screams
it looks like tears
it tastes like a dark room
covered in a blanket
with a Jerry Springer episode in the background
Teetering on the edges of consonants and vowels
"I'm sorry"s and I love u and all the unseen adjectives in
    the middle

i can't see out of this room
or this blanket
or the ache in between

But that room angst is only a dream
Cuz after u left us
i checked into the sidewalk motel
And if i look outside
All i see is the sides of your feet
When i try to sleep

Unhoused and UnLoved
Stuck in between life and death
And loss

Politricks and Poverty

Across this Stolen Land in this State of Emergency

Politricks and poverty—go together like milk and
    sour honey
Po folks used and abused for this politricks shell game—
"We just want to help them (by getting rid of them…
"We just want people to see there is still hope
"We have to get rid of the homeless problem—
"We have to build affordable housing

Who's the sweetest talking poverty pimps on the street?
People been selling poverty to get votes since politricks
    started
Easing the fascist itch of wanting to not see
Poverty—kinda like the krapitalist game of monopoly
Means about as much as the pink 10 dollar bills u tryna
    give me
So much bullshit—makes it hard to see
Yea its a wrap—just give me yo vote and i'll give u a house—
    or give them a house
or at least get them out of your town
Why didn't u do what you said? politrickster ted
oh that's right it was a lie—
but hey it made u feel good at the time….

From the PoemCast from a Poverty Skola Series…..written
in honor of my fellow poverty disabled unhoused and abused
skolaz—my fellow folks who are no longer considered human
cuz we outside—now just called the Homeless Problem by
politricksters across the United Snakes

On the Side of the Love-Road

Once upon a time there was a daughter of a mama with a
    fractured heart
who was a daughter of a mama with a broken heart
who was a daughter of a daughter with only a piece of
    a heart

these mamas and daughters held their broken hearts in
    their hands,
cut in so many places they almost couldn't be grasped—
slipping thru their broken fingers like sand, water, blood
    or air—

they taught each other cracked dreams of how not to be
    broken—
they walked thru life and mama-hood with nothing but
    blood drips and unclear desires for something that
    didn't hurt.

they fell into men and each other like it would end the
    break.endings
and the break-ups
ripping new tears into their chest.
their black and blue eyes would look out from black
    and blue lives.

Bruises felt like hope.
Slaps and cracked bones soothed the ache of alone.
violence was an ointment to rub on the bleeding scabs
    of loss.

they re-wrote horror stories as love stories—writing want
into every torn page.

one of the daughters thrown out of the love-car and left to
die on the side of the love-road
burning from the ache
holding onto a shard of maybes with one broken fingernail
erased with the terror of alone
precipice holding
woke up one day
realizing something that she wanted to be loved so bad that
she had made it love—
realizing that everything that loved her was already around
her and it didn't taste like blood or pain or loss
realizing that maybe
she wasn't
completely
broken
at all

Grant Dance / Had a Dream

Had a dream—
not to save the world
but to save other unhoused disabled mamaz & little girls

U see I was that baby wit my mama
holding that sign
the one you turned away from
pretending I wasn't alive

grew up wit mama—
her and me almost didn't make it thru the poverty/racism/
    houselessness drama
hustled for food—
never had the rent

until mama sed chase that dream—
write a grant—take a chance
u got skills tiny
U can do the grant dance

U see—we the Philathro-pimps
u a sexy young thing with at least one grant cycle we can
exploit
just come and sniff a little of this grant guidelines oil…

You can do whatever you want
(Darth Vader voice) BUT ALWAYS DO WHAT WE SAY

SO happy
created a job for my uncle, houseless friends and my
    momma

Wow—self-determination
liberation words, and dreams
helping each other

And then…
What?? you ain't doing what we say…
reporting on each other
Every time they late
Or miss an appointment
They miss three—oh well—they ass out of the grant stipend
That's dollars and sense poor mammas
We don't care if u got kids

keep those feet up—the philanthro-pimps say
that grant might run out
cuz, well, u ain't sexy anymore
—anyway

Dollar Signs for Eyes (Water is Life)

A Poem for Standing Rock (dedicated to all Water Protectors)

Water is life
but not to the colonized
who have lost their eyes
to dollar signs
deep in dark corners with bankkksters
mama earth hoarders
& blood-stained money lovers
covering our ancestors with
colonizer bricks & colonizer mortar
Water is life to us
the people who drink, love, & hold water
instead of blood-soaked dollars
—think love instead of kolonizer borders
who have mamaz & babies we care for
not merchandise we order
Water is life and
blue suits with dollar signs for heads say
"Not without a price"
We say water is life—
they say
it's water.. or your life
we drink poison & eat oil
& pray to corporations
& rub ourselves in your toil
& dream of how much more and more of mama earth
we can destroy
& people we can kill
& mamas lands we can devil-op and drill
Water is life—
and for those of us outside

drinking the man's poison wine
trying to hide in doorways, cardboard boxes and streetsides
on stolen land called public but not for us house-less
we beg for water on days so hot we might survive or not
hoping someone might give us a break
overstanding that for ALL of us
water is life—
And Our Great Mama is not here for the take

From CPS to ICE—the Separation Nation didn't begin with these Incarcerated Babies

The Violent Separation Nation didn't begin with this generation
with these babies
or their incarceration
The Separation Nation began with the theft of Turtle Island
and the humans who lived here and thrived on it

It continues today with the Confusion of age-grade
separated schools, Special Edukkkation and racist classist
Child Separation (Services)
predating on poor parents and parents of color

With people being encouraged to leave their peoples,
languages, spirit
and cultures who made them
with disabled children drugged against their human nature
with indigenous children ripped, violated, stolen and
abused from their families and nations

African children stolen from their mamas—so politricksters
and wealth-hoarders could hoard and amp up their profit-
making machinations

With mamas on HELL-FARE being considered Unfit and
Cut from their babies
because of poverty and the profit of the Charity
industrial system
the savior complex and the lie of best interests of the child

for the System that gives monies to foster care and
state-run homes
rather than poor mamas, poor families just trying to live
and thrive
with little to be alive

Please stay focused family on what matters now—
how this time of the hatchet man for the aristoKRAZY
CON-fusing us all

stay focused on the false borders
the false evictions
the buying and selling of our misery, bodies, Mama Earth
and all our generations

Mama was missing

#MMIW

A prayer poem—dedicated to all the missing, murdered
indigenous women—unhoused, unloved, broken,
forgotten—lost torn and in pieces—always thrown to the
bottom—

As a little girl My mama went missing—
looking out from a snapshot so small and dark
even the picture didn't listen
no one even knew or cared she was gone
mama always dreaming she wasn't here—so deeply alone
an Afro-Taino mixed race baby girl—no one wanted her
the child everyone wanted to lose—
a foster child no one wanted to choose
lost—not accidentally—always intentionally
cuz then it was one less mouth to feed—
one less brown body to see—
one less girl-child who wont come to b
not to have to forget—
her broken abused mama praying for my mama's death

For all the missing, murdered indigenous
      sister-mama-daughters
u know wut im saying fellow poverty skolaz
u know those mamaz and daughters lost in our herstories—
      all but forgotten
our mamaz mamas—unhoused, unloved
violently abused & always undone
our mamaz, our aunties, back and forth in sorrow
the women looking from the sides of life
cleaning your sheets, taking out your trash—

working for nothing day and night
washing your dishes & your clothes
taking care of your babies—
never her own
this prayer goes out to all the missing murdered indigenous
    women—to my houseless aunti abused & left on the side
    of the road
the ones we only see in our memories—
missing mamaz who have missing daughters who they said
    made bad choices
who they said don't matter
all the women u don't see—until they are just a number
something to march for—just a picture on a poster—

Miss you everyday mama

5150 Hold

Why did u leave me? Why did u leave and go away—taking my heart and throwing it in the goddam muthfukinwhor street—u are a whore—anyway, slept with Bush—iknowit i saw it—why did u leave MEEEEEE?

Her hair was long strands sailing in the night air with no people that wonder or care about her and only people who want her out of sight

"Dont touch her"—"dont speak "—"she is crazy"

5150 holds since she was 3

My mama—used to say— "one day that will be me"—if u leave me—i will b there screaming—pushing a shopping cart—begging the world to not hurt me—

and then there is a too young girl who walks the streets at night with only her shirt on screaming at a family who long ago left—and then the scream goes out to someone—the same one

for hours—until it is night—

will someone come for her—or will people just walk by disgusted and afraid—perpetuating the violent act of looking away?

u see i come from the rivers of broken people where our eyes leak sorrow and our faces melt with pain—and the city sprays water on our bodies and calls us out our name—and we are less important than recycled bottles and only worth the price that our incarceration can gain

Why did u leave me? Why did u leave and go away—taking my heart and throwing it goddam muthfukinwhor street—u are a whore—anyway, slept with bush—iknowit i saw it— why did u leave and go away?

These women and men blend into the night sky becoming a shadow from a moonbeam—a doorway or just a memory in your minds

screaming out to the human race for eternally failing us to the lie of independence and the violent act of looking away

Sister can u spare a crumb

(to the tune of "Brother Can You Spare a Dime")

They used to sell me on the amerikkan dream, and so I
    followed the mob,
When there were houses to clean, or shoes to shine, I was
    always there, right on the job.
They used to tell me bout the amerikan dream, work hard
    and you'll get ahead,
Why should I be standing, here in jail—incarcerated for not
    having a roof over my head?

Once I worked at walmart—in the checkout line—made it
    race against time
Once I worked at walmart now it's done.
Sister, can you spare a crumb?
Once I built a tower, up to the sun, brick, rivet, and lime;
Once I built a tower, now it's done.
Sister, can you spare a dime?

Now in orange jail suits, gee we look swell,
Full of that PIC smell,
Half a million women locked in this Hell,
And I was here wit my mom

Say, don't you remember, they called me nel;
it was nel all of the time.
Why don't you remember, I'm your pal?
Sister, can you spare a dime?

76

The look of Lies is in your eyes...

A PoemCast from a Poverty Skola for KrapitalisMas
(sung to the tune of "The Look of Love")

The look of Lies
is in
your eyes
That disguise you apply once a year for people like
mine
substance-addicted
screaming,
unhinged words
disheveled hair and clothes
Sterilized, terrorized...
us that you refer to as "those"
You give us a plate with
surgical gloves
and in that moment
you have absolved
the miles of lies of hoarded wealth
who has access to housing
and who can afford health

The look of lies
is in
your eyes
to ensure we don't have to touch
and there never has to be respect or love

Born inside the charity industry
Don't worry I'm not going to take more than you hand me
but i cannot promise to remind u this day was born on a
lie—

the lie of discovery
Missionary-crafted poverty
moving handily into the non-profit industry
to "deal" with people like me
in Poverty

So as i wait for my charity plate
This houseless chyle rewrites this sad state
and i resist the other-izing of my fate
u tear off the gloves and fake smile
and you break us off a piece of what was never yours
what u claim is entitled
the lie of who is poor and who is an immigrant—
who has resources and who has to be pimped
The look of lies is in your eyes…

This PoemCast from a Poverty Skola goes out on
krapitalistmas holiday to all of my fellow houseless/poor/
isolated single mama and daddies—children and elders—
lost in the separation-nation—that tells us we all need to be
FREE from the complicated—Independent and Away and
Done with that messy family—messy elders, and ghetto
poverty skolaz—done with all the prayer of our ancestors,
our love for mama earth and/or the songs from our elders
in church—from the Santos, the traditions you have all been
successfully taught away from because no one could make
money on

The indigenous cultures and languages that made u—and
then the krapitalism that CONfused u—to all of us all of
you—listen up—Interdependence isn't a cutesy idea or a
grant pimp guideline—it's real and complicated and takes
your precious time away from the krapitalist hamster wheel

of fake ass success—and one thing that Covid taught us even if we didn't want to learn it is how much we need each other—how much all those hugs matter—and that love matters—and how many lies were tied up in so-called krapitlist notions

Me and mama weren't just homeless because we were poor—disabled and traumatized—we were alone because people didn't want to deal with my mama and me—we were too complicated to overstand—too messy—too ghetto—and didn't fit into a charity stereotype—of helplessness—and anti-social work—didn't fit with scarcity charity—

As more and more people get told and sold solutions by academia and politricks—about how to help us without us—The Violence of Evictions and the ongoing Abuse called Sweeps, us revolutionary poor people remind u that we have our own solutions—that they have nothing to do with another akademik study, report, panel, kicked-down crumb but with long-term actual manifestable solutions & across the board—they are actually rooted in Interdependence— and all colonization stole from us—radical sharing of land and resources and skin that was never ours/yours in the first place—breaking us off for real—helping us with us and enacting the solution called ComeUnity Reparations

The Turkey and Mashed Potatoes Line

The Other KrapitalisMas Story

Once upon a time I stood in that turkey and mashed
potatoes salvation army line
begged for a bit of your once-a-year love
held onto mamas hand—even tho touch wasn't anything u
felt, knew or understand

her an untouched, unloved, mixed race houseless orphan
barely knew safety much-love love, hugs or kisses as a baby

it was like we weren't looking for love—but just somewhere
the pain might not be—

this time of year was beyond sick—
rage would overtake her
rage against what was never there—
deep sorrow to follow

the people who hurt her lined up
in an imaginary jail
from teachers to peers to so-called foster parents

barely came out of all that alive—
with PTSD so bad it didn't even have a start time

i inherited her everything—her beautiful deep spirit that
never gave up and almost untouchable pain that had no
end time
we struggled every day just to survive—not just food-less,
rent-less, houseless—but family-less—people-less—and
always so much alone—

Alone time—pour into fake notions of togetherness and connectedness that never was ours—Screams began on thanksTaking and didn't end till after gregorian new year time

Screams, moans of lost love—poured into with more krapitalist poverty than one human could hold—
Yes we made it—barely alive holding onto each other without words—just a tethered rope called we got to survive

This PoemCast for a poverty skola goes out to all the peoples holding the sorrows of a thousand rivers and the untouchable pain of the holidaze—the notion of PTSD and what it looks like for so many in this occupied mama earth filled with confusion and sorrow and wealth-hoarding and love-hoarding and trying to survive by any means necessary just to survive—

So this is a love poem for all who are listening—a love poem of consciousness—to hold onto yourselves, your babies—
to practice a hug and kiss even if u aren't used to it—to appreciate that you lived with this trauma this long—realize if u made it this far u are already alright—that to survive PTSD is to shine and that at least to know that this poverty skola hopes and holds u in a a great big almost smile that healing and so-called self-care isn't always so easy when u still unsure of how to feel yourself—that healing and change is slow—that it will come and for now the pain is real too—so love that in you—even if its a lot of the time—and guess what family—it's gonna be alright—it's gonna be alright—

EBT I'm yo baaadest B

(to "Double Cross - Hard Freestyle Trap Beat,"
youtu.be/fW2flBSkv1M)

EBT—u got me
EBT—u got me
EBT—best believe
I'm yo baaadest b
Sell my azz for crums like these

EBT—EBT
U already know
I'm deep in poverty—
Can't you see
I'm yo best ho
Don't ya know

Back on the street
But u all I need—
U my govt daddy—
I know u really love me—

So I take those hits—
Medi-cal pimp—be hard on this chick

I don't got no side kick
U say I'm lying if I don't cough up EVERY trick
Hit me wit yo hate
knock me out
wit yo govt cheese plate—

No matter how many of yo PROOF OF INCOME FORMS

U STILL SAY—I'M LYING—I'M HIDING
force me into trafficking more of yo po' people porn

Prove you live here—prove that's u
I got more & more for u to do
R u really living in your home
Show me bills—show me ID
Show me when u went to the corner sto
and then when I think we finally ready
U throw another bait and switch—
give me another form
to prove I'm really yo bitch

EEEEEEBBBBTTT—u got me
Pls don't
Pls not
Pls don't—
Pls don't hi me
I didn't do it
I didn't lie—
I'm just tryin to get some food and medical care time

So I come back
I got 329 pages of paperwork
To prove all that
To show u I'm working hard
I aint messin with no one else
All my forms are yours daddy

U my one & only
it's only Calfresh for me baby

I'm Yo Client—Service-Resistant and Non-Compliant

I'm your patient, consumer client
service-resistant, difficult and non-compliant
whatever acronym
u can write it down in my PHAT file
I'm all those things u call me
Every time u try to Case Mangle my broken poverty

Send out your anti-social workers, poLICE
politricksters and Eeeee Dee's

Whatever crumbs u dole out
I won't bow down
There will b new laws to criminalize my unhoused body
this is without a doubt
standing in your poor people bread lines,
squatting in your rich people hospital beds
getting your cash crumbs that don't begin to feed me, see
     me or ever heal me or mines

but I'm still here
yelling, calling
fighting, screaming epithets
Filing legal papers like my Po' skola brother charles pitts
never taking ISH
from non-profiteers
to poverty pimps
from Foundations to
to the Grant Pimp Nation
speaking up for everyone

who doesn't want to hear my
difficult azz shit

Yea I'll be yelling at your politrickster door
meanwhile building, manifesting—poor people's solutions
to your ongoing poverty industry horror
of scarcity models
and the deserving versus undeserving poor

Yea—keep marginalizing us broken and fighting back poor
cuz every time u look away we building, creating—and Still
    Fighting for our Rights at
YOUR DOOR!!!

Cages for Sages

Poverty and Wite Supremacy created these cages and
     these cagers
these guns & these tasers
Cages for sages
So they can quiet the rages
against poor peoples' scarcity models, racism, poverty and
     lack of housing—

And all the things
They are saving
For krapitalist saviors to swoop in and save us

How bout we create, lift up and love up
Our own pages
Of spirit & culture
And thrival

Of jailhouse lawyering
And poor peoples' survival
And Unpack the
The lies of the master and the slaver
How bout we realize we all had it here before them
And we don't need their parole plans
And their stolen land, false borders and bans
And their continued enslavement

How bout we stop—
Listen to Mama Earth
And the land under this stolen rock
That gives us all we need
Outside of the lies of Krapitalist greed

The herstories and gifts of our indigenous ancestors
Is all we need
And our minds to get clear
Who the terrorist is here
and the real Gangs are banksters who wear white collars &
    count Bloodstained dollars cuz of toxic greed—
And the wealth-hoarders right around us calling the PoLice
And all of you beautiful brothers and sisters are it—
And to listen to Poor Peoples' Theory—cuz we have our
    own ancestors' knowledge and gifts
Like Free Aztlan, KAGE universal and George Jackson and
    Poverty Scholarship
Krapitlism is a lie family—
And it will die with them—
IT will die with Cage-creating—Lies-perpetrating—Stolen-
    land-dominating—greed-hoarding—Old Wite Men—

Stop Calling—(the poLice)

Stop Callin'
Stop Stallin'
Stop Talking while more Black and Brown Suns and
    daughters are fallen

No I mean Stop enabling and Kolonizing
a system that kills
more than it ever cures our ills
with roots in the original theft of Turtle island
Meant to CONfuse our already CONfused mindSets

Got us all believing that numbers like 911 mean housed
people are safe from us houseless—that witesAndLites are
safe in their own embedded desire for wealth-hoarding
wite-ness

that continuing to buy & evict, foreclose, sweep, and kick—
    makes anyone safe from myths
About how to be safe and what is the way to handle fear and
    danger everyday
In a place already stolen
A land already rife with murderous lies that keep getting
    told and sold

That Was set up to Shoot, Kill every Black, Brown or poor
    person in their way
Was locked in to support fear
so more protected classes could steal
And more of us could end up in their jail cells

These are the legacies of the Stealing Fathers And the
    Kop-callers
And the way to unlink us Po' from the Lice
Is for you to stop and think
Why am I calling—
And how did I begin to believe The LIE
that safety ever meant dialing
9-!-!
leading to the death of more
black, brown and poor daughters and Suns.

Living Poverty Pimp-Free

Dedicated to all warriors for Decolonization from this
web of lies... thx for NEVER giving up the fight!

Living pimp-free
is not eas-y
because to be really, truly free
is to be without
the security

Of systems in place,
To secure and displace,
to create fakely named safe space,
With simple answers to hard questions
Like violence and hate,
Poverty and race

U see—
to live Pimp free
Is to deconstruct ALL the capitalist realities
Of poLice, Politricks, NPIC, and white supremacy

To recognize how so few peoples got all that stolen money,
trading on false borders, prisons and indigenous peoples'
liberty

And to live Poverty Pimp–free—
To really be truly free—
Is to redesign systems based on eldership, ancestors,
     Pachamama
And We

To deconstruct all the simple answers of why
we kill each other,
starve our mothers,
shoot and kill our Black, Brown and houseless sisters and
    brothers
incarcerate so many others

To walk through lyfe Poverty Pimp–free
is to stop, look, listen and see—
Move off the grid of control, share resources, with
    each other—
Teach ourselves and our children
Build our own self-determined housing—
create our own work and jobs
Barter with each other
Launch reparations of blood-stained amerikkkan dollaz

Reach out and touch
Connect with, repair and love
All of us—

Without a step and fetch it hustle—
But with the decolonized truth—
even if it hurts, confuses, takes time
and means more "trouble"

U see
to live pimp-free IS the revolution
In a 21st century corporate 1%-led Aristocracy

So here I am in my dreams
riding pimp-free
Slanging elders' knowledge instead of what they charge u for

in eugenecist kkkollege
Scolding, holding and caring for mamaz, babies and elders,
Marching, protesting, praying and acting against devil-
opers, sacred site desecrators, bank-pimps, corporate
pimps and poLice killers
Bartering food, starting our children good,
Listening to our ancestors, caring and praying for our mama
Taking the lessons even when they are filled with drama-
Trying, not dying, to live, to give, to dream, to see—a life for
all of us—that is truly
Pimp-free

We ain't there yet—but Creator knows—
It will someday be...
a life—
that is truly Poverty Pimp–free...

There is a House in East Huchiun...

(To the soundz of "There is a House in New Orleans")

There is a house in East Huchiun
They Call it Homefulness
And it's been the dream of many a poor girl
And God I know i'm one

My mama was disabled
Tortured as a child
My father was a rich wite man
Who left us all to die

Now the only thing a poor mama needs
Are hands to hold her broken dreams
But mama and me were all alone
So instead we lived hidden on the street

mama and me were broken
Barely made it out alive
but no matter what
She refused to believe in the
settler colonial lies

Sometimes the pain is too hard
Mama said I can't go on
But walk this change
On this Ohlone land
And Build us all a home

Well there is a house in East Huchiun
They call it Homefulness

And it's been the hope of many a poor girl & boy
And GOD I know we are them

Well there is a house in East Huchiun
They call HOMEFULNESS
And it's been the dream of many a poor boy & girl
And god I know we are them

PoShunary
(The Po' People's Dictionary)

Cause we can't use the kkkolonizers words to liberate
ourselves, our ancestors and our MamaEarth

Akkkademia / akkkademiks — most if not all of the institutions of higher "learning" across Turtle Island were built by land-stealers, wealth-hoarders and colonizers. Most of the buildings on their "campuses" are named after eugenicists, or people that actively promoted, supported or benefited off of pure race science and/or the theft of land, lives, bodies, knowledge and culture across Mama Earth.

AristoKrazy — Wealth-Hoarders/Land-stealers who believe that they know more inherently, because of their "bloodlines" of privilege and so-called wealth, about survival, thrival, use of resources and Mama Earth and life itself

AnthroWrongOlogy and Arkkkaeology — The theft, storage, display, removal, and displacement of indigenous ancestors, poor, Black and Brown people for study, research, profit, entertainment or devil-opment without the descendants' inclusion, permission, leadership, direction, prayer protocol, and/or ceremony.

Anti-Social Work & Case Manglers — The angry-at-poor-people, working-for-the-man, believing-in-the-"sys," hegemony-filled people who often work in the non-profit industrial complex as front-line staff or advocates, or in Social Security, welfare/Hellfare offices, shelters or drop-in centers and ascribe to the scarcity model of the "deserving vs. undeserving poor" notion that poor people are lazy, crazy, etc.—which is often translated/taught in training sessions, academia, and/or existent in a person who lacks poverty scholarship.

AMON-stazon — (remix of Amazon) as it has become a literal monster, "owning," destroying, buying, selling ideas, art, life, and our Mama Earth

Blood-Stained Dollars: US Dollars or Euros (and all other empire monetary systems) gained off the exploitation, wars, removal and/or genocide of people.

Brother-Ship/Sister-Ship/Mama-Ship — The opposite of a "fellow-ship"— a designation, support for loving and caregiving for your family, community and village.

CONfused CONsumer — using billion-dollar ad campaigns to "sell" happiness and love and so-called sexiness to people, resulting in people associating love with material things in a kkkrapitalist system. Side effects/impacts—hoarding/cluttering illness, the lie of "credit," bankruptcy and the violence of debt

CorpRape / CorpRapeShun — remix of "corporate/corporation" as these entities exist to extract, destroy, desecrate, kill, poLice and profit off of poor, indigenous, Black and Brown peoples, animals, Mama Earth, Mama Ocean and her resources, Air, Water, Land and resources

ComeUNITY — A village of poor/indigenous and/or in-struggle folks operating interdependently.

Eldership — The active (as opposed to passive and in name only), non-capitalist practice of caring for, honoring, and showing deference to elders in your family and in society.

Folks in Struggle — We don't say "homeless people," as if "homeless" were our only identity just because we don't have access to a roof. "Homeless" is a grant-pimp guideline word/determination. We don't say "low-income"—because whose idea of low-income are we talking about within a capitalist society? And we don't even always say "in poverty," because that isn't the only way to describe the struggle of people who struggle with other oppressions like racism, ableism, gender oppression, border fascism, and more. So, as often as we can, we say "folks in struggle" instead, adding that folks are in struggle with poverty, ableism, houselessness, landlessness, and more.

GentriFUKation — Gentrification and displacement of poor peoples of color and indigenous peoples from their rooted communities, jobs, and land.

Hellthcare — The treatment received (or not received) by poor, unhoused, disabled, migrant/immigrant, indigenous and/or very low-income people.

Houseless/Landless/Unhoused — As poverty skolaz we resist the term "homeless." Like "youth" and "seniors," "homeless" is another way that nonprofit industrial complex organizations, philanthro-pimped grants, legislators, politicians, corporate governments, media, and akkkademics "separate" us from the tables of decision-making and power, so they can talk about us instead of talking with us. By claiming the term "landless," we align ourselves with landless peoples movements in Brazil, Kenya, South Africa, and Mexico. Our relationship to a roof does not define us as people—we are multi-layered, multi-generational, multi-cultural, multi-racial, multi-lingual—we just don't have a roof—also many folks live outside in a neighborhood, community or town, that doesn't mean that we are any less residents than someone with access to a roof on this stolen, indigenous land.

Interdependence — The intentional connectedness of people, families, and community. Interdependence is the reliance on each other with an open acceptance that, as people, we need each other. It is a rejection of the bootstraps, capitalist ideal of separateness, isolation, and western, Euro-centric ideas of individuation and independence.

Homefulness — a homeless, landless, self-determined movement solution to homelessness (currently being manifested in Deep East Occupied Huchiun)

KlanMark — So-called landmarks like Mount Rushmore and the Alamo (and so many more all across occupied Turtle Island) where colonial terror and colonial terrorists who stole Mama Earth, enslaved people and perpetuated genocide on indigenous, Black, Brown and Disabled bodies are held up as "leaders," "thinkers," artists, visionaries, scientists and "presidents"

kkKrapitalism/Krapitalist — a person of any culture or melanin who believes that the harming system of "capitalism" is our way to be "free," rooted in violent exploitation of your fellow human, mama earth resources or activity. Krapitalism is a word I created to clarify the racist classist, violent system known as Capitalism

KkkrapitalisMas — a day wrongly associated with the born-day of the revolutionary indigenous, melanted man known as Yeshua (Jesus) so that kkkrapitalists could make billions of dollars of bloodstained dollars in the CONsumer kkkrapitalist industry

Lie-gislators / Politricksters — The people known as legislators and politicians who use bloodstained and stolen dollars and power to abuse, criminalize and profit off of the backs of poor peoples and people of color. These folks should not be confused with conscious peoples who try to be in the race, classed and colonized space of politricks navigating the settler-colonizer laws for collective justice.

Linguistic Domination: Linguistic domination privileges the colonizers' languages and speech, which results in the exclusion, shame, silencing, segregation, disempowerment, and destruction of voices speaking their indigenous languages and tongues. Proficiency in the colonizers' tongues affords access, space, resources, and power to a small group of people with race, class, and/or educational privilege. Linguistic domination rewards people who can master not only the master's language but also the dominant way of thinking, forming ideas, and living. These institutionalized forms of silencing dictate which words and information are considered legitimate, who and what is funded to create media, and who is considered valid as an expert, a media maker, a communicator. The colonizers' languages have been afforded this legitimacy and "privilege" via access to stolen resources and imperialistic stability— e.g. libraries, endowments, institutions of academia, media corporations, and the like.

MiddleClassMedia Missionary (MCMM) — Media creators who have, as my Mama Dee would say, never missed a meal (in other words no poverty scholarship) and do "exposés" on marginalized peoples and communities with the idea that by telling our stories for us without us they are "helping" us. Writing about us poor and houseless peoples with no accountability to us or inclusion of our voices, a media missionary is silencing the peoples and communities they purport to help. Like all missionary work, media-missionary work is misguided; the "help" can be a form of genocide, telling a story that's not the media-maker's to tell, leading to/enabling the destruction of a community. Media-missionary work is not specific to corporate media, but it started there.

Media Resistance — Media resistance occurs when people who are usually intentionally silenced by media channels create media for the purposes of change, resistance, and revolution.

Non-Profiteers & the Savior Industrial Complex — Non-profiteers—in the tradition of capitalist paper-theft projects like real estate, multinational corporations, hedge funds, and fake insurance policies based on "capital" earned on long-ago-stolen land. Nonprofit organizations are created as corporations, beginning with 501(c)3 papers that use language very similar to that of for-profit corporations. They are all created with capitalist, individualistic structures like boards, secretaries, and presidents who follow strict guidelines and codes of conduct meant to "keep everything in line." The organizations function in the same way corporations do—sometimes even worse, depending on what they do. Big poverty-pimped organizations like

Goodwill and Salvation Army compete for government contracts to "provide" services to poverty, disability, youth, and migrant skolaz and then create large shelters that operate like jails, with piss tests and shut-down rules. Smaller organizations insist that we respect "boundaries" and create punitive requirements/actions if we don't follow the "rules"—which often means that we are punished for acting in the ways of our ancestors, with indigenous love and respect. Nonprofits within the Nonprofit Industrial Complex (NPIC) create projects based on the "guidelines" of big philanthro-pimps, which leads to separatist, individualistic ways of allegedly providing services. In reality, though, they keep people sick, in the system, and out of control.

Philanthro-Pimping — The industry of philanthropy includes a heavy pimping aspect with covert and overt ways of commodifying and exploiting people and their pain, struggle, and oppression. This process of commodification and exploitation often includes language about the "sexiness" of a project, initiative, or problem. See Chapter 10 of *Poverty Scholarship: Poor People-Led Theory, Art, Words & Tears Across Mama Earth.*

Po'Lice — Paid agents of the prison industrial complex (PIC) who protect property and provide customers for the PIC.

Povertyskola — a person who has struggled with homelessness, poverty, eviction, false borders, racism, incarceration, profiling and/or other forms of colonial oppression in this stolen land.

Poor Peoples' Equity — Within a capitalist context, equity means the falsely bolstered property values of stolen land acquired through paper theft. Within a context of landless/ houseless people, though, it can mean many things: fair access to a roof that we aren't at risk of being kicked out of due to non-payment or lack of access to blood-stained amerikkkan dollaz (which landless/houseless people never have, due to many racist and classist setups and paper thefts and boundaries and dominations that happen every day to poor people/indigenous peoples); the ability to walk into a store and not have a security guard follow you; access to mental health services; the knowledge that someone is caring for you or will care for you if you are an elder; relationships, from academic networks to knowing there are people you can count on to provide a job or a place to stay, or anything else. Equity is covert, intangible, and at the root of race and class separation.

Poor Peoples' Sweat Equity — Access to land, housing, and food security, not based on how many bloodstained amerikkkan dollaz we have or the over-used and oftentimes ableist, racist and classist concept of "sweat equity" based on how much physical labor humans can do. Poor peoples' sweat equity is based on "whatever we can do" as poor elders, youth, disabled and differently abled poor people, i.e., child care, media, chairing of meetings, cleaning, organizing, i.e., the time, love, sweat, labor, struggle, and spirit we put into caring for our mama, each other and Pachamama.

Real E-Snakes & Devil-opers — Real-estate snakkkes and developers are the people or organizations who imagine and oversee real-estate speculation, from conceptualizing new real-estate developments to buying land to financing and managing construction to selling and leasing. Most developers are devil-opers, key agents of community destruction and displacement. When a developer uses "redevelopment" of an area to destroy and displace a thriving community of color, they get statues and plazas named after them. For example, Justin Herman, head of San Francisco's Redevelopment Agency in the 1960s, oversaw the displacement of tens of thousands of people of color from a neighborhood that was once described as the nation's most diverse. That neighborhood now has a plaza named after him. See also gentriFUKation.

Underground Economic Strategies — Unrecognized ways of work, labor, and business such as selling products on the streets without a license or selling services not seen as "legal" or sanctioned by society. Underground economic strategists include recyclers, panhandlers, and unlicensed street vendors or artists.

Amerikkklan — The Stolen indigenous territory of Turtle Island named after one of the colonizers who aided and abetted in the stealing of this land and building/creating the mythology of discovery.

WeSearch — I launched the concept of We-Search because I don't believe in the akkkademic domination of research. Academic research uses philanthro-pimped and funded initiatives to study, deconstruct, and survey poor youth, adults, and elders in struggle. This research creates papers, thesis projects, and studies that talk about how poor we are, how much racism there is, and how bad our neighborhoods and schools are. We-Search is poor-people-led research and proactive media that deconstructs the lies told about our criminalized and mythologized communities.

Wite — Not to be confused with the "color" or the melanin in someone's skin, this relates to the system of "White supremacy" that rules institutions of learning, housing, hellthcare and service provision in the US.

Wite-Science — Post-colonial science, medicine, biology, eugenics, rooted in/based on the study, experimentation, torture, exploitation and/or death of indigenous, Black, Brown, Disabled peoples stolen, disrespected, poisoned, incarcerated bodies.

I hope u are writing a poem

I hope u are writing a poem—
to sew together the skin next to my bones
in the empty places where my heart should be
and where instead betrayal lurks
and my broken eyes can't even see

I hope u r writing yourself out of the selfie-absorption river
and souls-less neglect
to sew back this broken rabbit's neck
I hope verse is flowing between well-crafted words
of so-called revolution murmurs
and inconvenient slurs

I hope u r writing something to the one who u supposedly
loved even if it's hard
cuz I'm clean out of trust—
collecting tears in a tiny jar—

Author Bio

Tiny (aka Lisa Gray-Garcia) is a formerly unhoused, incarcerated poverty scholar, revolutionary journalist, lecturer, poet, visionary, teacher and single mama of Tiburcio, daughter of a houseless, disabled, indigenous mama Dee, and the co-founder of POOR Magazine/Prensa POBRE/PoorNewsNetwork. She is the author of *Criminal of Poverty: Growing Up Homeless in America*; co-editor of *A Decolonizers Guide to A Humble Revolution*, *Born & Raised in Frisco*, and *Poverty Scholarship: Poor People Theory, Arts, Words and Tears Across Mama Earth*, which was released in 2019; co-author of *How to Not Call the Po'Lice Ever* and *The Po' People's Survival Guide thru COVID-19 and the Virus of Poverty*; and author of the children's books *The Hard Worker (Trabajador Fuerte)* and *When Mama and Me Lived Outside*, with protagonists struggling with homelessness, gentrification, and po'Lice terror.

In 2011 she co-launched The Homefulness Project—a landless/homeless peoples, self-determined land liberation movement in the occupied Ohlone/Lisjan/Huchiun territory known as Deep East Oakland, with spiritual guidance and permission from Lisjan leaders, and co-founded a liberation school for children, Deecolonize Academy, and a revolutionary Poor peoples-led Radio station and press of the same name, POOR Press. She has conceived, co-written, workshopped and performed theatre with fellow poor and homeless people including the welfareQUEENS, Hotel Voices and PovertySkolaz plays for the stage. Her podcast series, *PoemCast from a Poverty Skola*, is available on Spreaker, iTunes and more. To find her work, go to www.lisatinygraygarcia.com.

Made in the USA
Monee, IL
09 May 2022